Lester B. Pearson

#14

The geek who made Canada proud

Written by Gordon R. Gibb

Illustrated by Susan N. Stewart

Photo Credits
JackFruit Press would like to thank the
Canadian National Archives for images
appearing on pages 9 (C-018704), 13 (PA-
110824), 17 (PA-119892), 23 (PA-110827),
and 39 (PA-117097).

© 2006 JackFruit Press Ltd.
Publisher—Jacqueline Brown
Editor—Annie Jacobsen
Series Editor—Helen Waumsley
Designer and Art Director—Marcel Lafleur
Researcher—Barbara Baillargeon, Hagit
Hadaya, and Peter Konieczny

JackFruit Press Ltd.
Toronto, Canada
www.jackfruitpress.com

Library and Archives Canada Cataloguing in
Publication

Gibb, Gordon R., 1957–
Lester B. Pearson: The geek who made
Canada proud / written by Gordon R. Gibb;
illustrated by Susan N. Stewart.

(Canadian prime ministers: warts and all)
Includes index.

ISBN 0-9736406-2-6

1. Pearson, Lester B., 1897–1972–Juvenile
literature. 2. Prime ministers–Canada–Biog-
raphy–Juvenile literature. 3. Canada–Politics and government–1963–1968–Juvenile
literature. I. Stewart, Susan N. II. Title. III.
Series.

FC621.P4G53 2006
j971.064'3092   C2006-901629-1

Printed and bound in Canada

. . . So, I'm here to show you around this really cool series of books on great Canadians.

This book tells the story of Lester B. Pearson, Canada's 14th prime minister.

He had a high, chirpy voice and spoke with a lisp, but when he talked peace, the whole world listened!

Contents

Hot topics

Mike Pearson: The hero

Mike has an image problem. Most Canadians have no idea what a great man their 14th prime minister is. They either don't know or don't remember that he has been president of the United Nations. They don't realize that he saved the world from what could have been a major war. Or that he came up with the idea of creating a multinational army to keep the peace all over the globe.

Canada's 14th prime minister came to power at the wrong time. Radio and television were just beginning to make a difference in what people thought of their leaders—and for Lester B. Pearson, that was bad news.

He was smart and very knowledgeable. He was athletic and well-connected in the world of **international diplomacy**. His friends loved him. His business contacts respected him. Many world leaders looked up to him.

But most ordinary Canadians had no idea what a great man he was. That's because Lester had an image problem: he was not as he appeared to be. When he spoke in public, he often sounded hesitant, unsure of what he wanted to say. Worse, he had a high, chirpy voice that made it hard for strangers to take him seriously.

An image problem

Even his 16-year-old daughter knew her father had an image problem. She realized it the first time she heard him give a speech on the radio. She wrote to him and said, "Gee, Daddy, you have a lisp!" She was right. At his worst, Lester sounded like Elmer Fudd, the bumbling hunter from the Bugs Bunny cartoons. That his name was Lester certainly didn't help. Neither did his image as a bookworm, nor his fondness for bow ties. People who didn't know him might have been tempted to call him a geek.

Yet Lester was everything but. People who knew him personally knew he was definitely not a bookworm or a social misfit. In fact, he was somewhat of a jock and a bit of a sports hero. He'd played semi-professional baseball for the Guelph Maple Leafs, hockey for Oxford University, and was an outstanding lacrosse player. He'd also played basketball, rugby, squash, tennis, road hockey, cricket, and golf—once with an unexploded bomb on the fairway.

Mike or Lester?

In **World War I**, when Lester was training to become a pilot, his flight instructor decided the name "Lester" was uncool, so he gave him the nickname "Mike." Fortunately, Lester liked being called Mike, and the new name stuck. Mike went on to survive an airplane crash and a collision with a double-decker bus during a blackout in London. Later on, he became a well-known diplomat trusted with top-secret missions. His personal commitment to peace, together with his down-to-earth personality and cheerful optimism, inspired the confidence of world leaders and many Canadians. During his time at the **United Nations**, he helped stop a serious war. For this, he won the **Nobel Peace Prize**.

But for a man of peace, Mike sure had to face some serious challenges. His time as prime minister was exciting because it spanned the **Vietnam War**, the threat of Quebec separating from Canada, and the celebration of Canada's centennial. At one point, the representative of a women's group threatened that a million women would march on **Parliament Hill** if his government didn't start reforms to end discrimination against women. Mike built a bilingual **civil service**, **medicare**, and the **Canada Pension Plan**. He also introduced loans for university and college students. In the middle of all this, Mike had the guts to challenge tradition by giving Canada an important symbol you may have thought we'd always had: our Maple Leaf flag.

Not bad for a "geek"

Mike had few enemies in his lifetime. Prime Minister **William Lyon Mackenzie King** talked about "the light which shone through him." He was a diplomat who hated squabbling, and yet a major part of his job as prime minister was dealing with conflicting views every single day. He sometimes failed to support his **cabinet ministers** when they needed his help. And he wasn't strong in politics, especially when he had to deal with money and business.

In spite of all that, Mike Pearson will be remembered as an international man of peace who won for Canada the reputation of being a helpful, friendly, peace-loving people. Not bad for a "geek," eh?

Want to know more? The words in bold are explained in the glossary at the back of the book.

Lester has an image problem: he looks like something he's not. When he speaks in public, he can sound hesitant, unsure of what he wants to say. Worse, he has a high, chirpy voice that makes it hard for people to take him seriously.

Patricia, Lester's 16-year-old daughter, knows her father has an image problem. She realizes it the first time she hears him give a speech on the radio. She writes to him and says, "Gee, Daddy, you have a lisp!" She's right. At his worst, Lester sounds like Elmer Fudd from the Bugs Bunny cartoons.

Lester Pearson's grandfather is a gentle man whose motto is "live and let live." He's also a sports fan who can't get enough of baseball.

Dominion Day is lovely and sunny. Lester takes his grandfather to a doubleheader at Hanlan's Point on the Toronto Islands. After the morning's game, they decide to stay for lunch. And then it only makes sense to take in the second game. When they finally get home to their worried family, they're in big trouble. But they don't care—it's all been worth it.

Chapter 1
The preacher's kid

Lester Bowles Pearson was born on April 23, 1897, in Newtonbrook, Ontario, a small village north of Toronto. The road now known as Yonge Street went right through Newtonbrook; later the town became part of North York.

Lester's ancestors were Irish. His father's family originally came from Dublin and his mother's family came from Kilkenny in 1826.

Lester was the middle brother of three boys. His brother Duke was three years older, and Vaughn was a year younger. Lester's father, Edwin, and his grandfather, Marmaduke, were both Methodist ministers. His mother, Anne Bowles, a strong-minded woman, ran the family home and took care of her three active boys. Anne's father, a sheriff, was also a part-time minister. The Bowles family were farmers; the Pearsons were ordained ministers. Both families were very jolly, very Irish, yet strict when it came to right and wrong.

The Pearson boys grew up in a disciplined but loving home. Their father was a gentle man loved by his parishioners. His motto was "live and let live." He was also a sports fan, like his own father. Both of them loved baseball. Couldn't get enough of it. On **Dominion Day**, 1913, Lester took his grandfather (who was getting old and not moving around too well) to a doubleheader at Hanlan's Point on the Toronto Islands. It was a beautiful day, so, after the morning's game, they decided to stay for lunch. After lunch, it only made sense to take in the second game. When they finally got home to their worried family, they were in big trouble. But they didn't care; it had been worth it.

1897
Lester is born on April 23.

1898
His brother, Vaughn, is born.

1913
Lester graduates from high school and starts at the University of Toronto.

1914
World War I begins. His older brother Duke enlists in the army.

1915
Lester joins the Canadian Army Medical Corps on his 18th birthday.

Like a lot of kids his age, Lester wasn't sure what he wanted to be when he grew up. But one of his diaries gives us a clue. He wrote about the time his uncle was elected mayor of Orangeville.

Everyone gathered at his uncle's house afterwards to celebrate. There was even a live band! Mike wrote, "This was true glory, and I concluded right there and then to become a politician so I could be a mayor and have a band play outside my house."

Lester was seen as a model child, unlike his brother Duke, who was the rascal of the family. Once, when everyone went up to the front of the church to pray, Lester stayed kneeling after the others had got up to go back to their seats. The adults were pretty impressed with Lester's devotion—until they realized he'd fallen fast asleep at the front!

School, sports, and church

Life for the Pearson boys was a combination of school, sports, and church. Because their father was a minister, they went to church a lot. A typical Sunday included baseball at 10 a.m., church at 11, Sunday school at 2:30, and an evening service at 7 p.m. TV hadn't been invented yet, and the Pearson boys weren't allowed to go to the movies—that is, until someone noticed that the owner of the local theatre contributed generously when the collection plate came around in church. Movies at the time were black and white and instead of the actors speaking, written words flashed across the screen. A piano player in the theatre provided the music.

The family moved often because many churches have a policy of moving their ministers from parish to parish every few years. Fortunately, all of the family's moves were in Ontario. From Newtonbrook, Lester moved to Davisville, also in the Toronto area, then to Peterborough, Aurora, and Hamilton. The Pearsons especially liked Peterborough. They lived in a house on Water Street, across from what is now the police station. Lester was a student at Central Public School. Math was one of his worst subjects. He also had a tough time in science and sometimes had to work hard just to pass. His favourite subjects were English, grammar, Latin, and history. While he lived in Hamilton, he had a newspaper route and got up at 6 every morning to deliver the *Toronto World*.

The war to end all wars

In 1913, after graduating from Hamilton Collegiate Institute at the age of 16, he went to Victoria College at the University of Toronto, the same college his father had attended. His brother, Duke, was studying there too, and they both played on the basketball team.

In the summer of 1914, he went home to Chatham, where his parents now lived, and played second base for a team in the Chatham City Baseball League.

On August 4, World War I began. Duke enlisted. Many young men were joining the army, feeling grown up and brave to be going off to war. Everyone was proud of our soldiers. Bands played. Parades marched. The atmosphere was festive. In their flashy uniforms, those 18-, 19-, and 20-year-olds looked like perfect gentlemen. No one had any idea that they were marching straight into a hell that would last for four years.

Like every other young man, Lester wanted to join, but his parents said no. They felt that, at 17, he was far too young to go to war. Besides, they said, he was enjoying university, studying hard and playing baseball and hockey. But there was a war going on and Canada was in it. War was in all the newspapers and was all that people talked about. Lester wanted to fight for his country. One day a friend told him there was a spot in the Canadian Army Medical Corps. On his 18th birthday, Lester rushed down to the recruiting office and signed up. Now he was Lester B. Pearson, private #1059.

War is in all the newspapers. It's all that people talk about. When a friend tells Lester there is a spot in the army medical corps, he rushes out to enlist on his 18th birthday.

1915

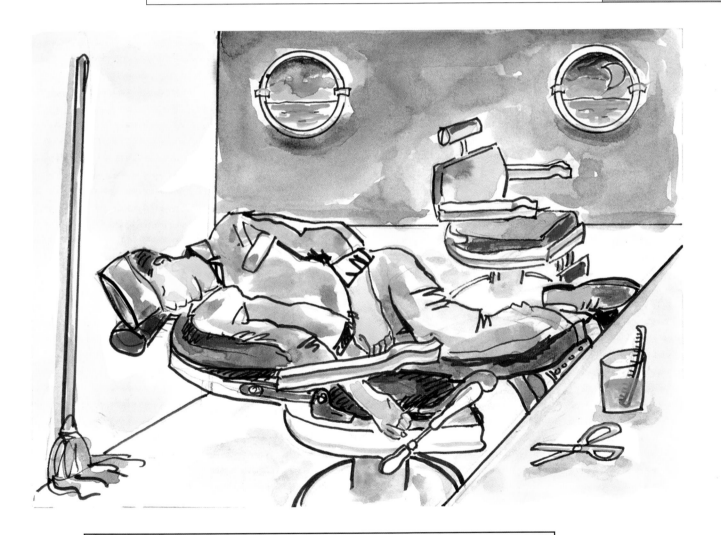

Private #1059 is shipped out of Montreal to Egypt. During the trip, he's both seasick and homesick and finds it impossible to sleep in his berth. He gets creative and pays the ship's barber to let him sleep in a padded barber chair at night.

Pilot training normally takes a year. But there is such a desperate need that Mike gets only two hours of instruction. He has to fly by himself and has no time to be afraid—until the moment comes to land . . .

Mike is so scared, he keeps flying until his plane is almost out of fuel. He doesn't crash, but for the rest of his life, he'll be sick to his stomach whenever he has to fly.

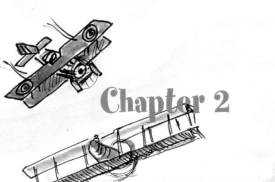

Chapter 2

Private Pearson longs for action

1915
Lester travels by ship to Egypt, where he works at a camp hospital, and then to Salonika as an orderly in a field hospital.

1917
Lester goes to England to train as a fighter pilot.

Lester was shipped out of Montreal to Egypt. During the trip, he was both seasick and homesick and found it impossible to sleep in the uncomfortable ship's bed. So he got creative and paid the ship's barber to let him sleep in the padded barber chair at night.

When the **corps company** landed, the adventure Lester had longed for didn't happen. He worked as a night orderly at a camp hospital, helping the doctors and comforting wounded soldiers. The best part was sitting at the foot of their beds listening to their heroic stories of the battlefield. He also worked in the camp store where soldiers got their supplies of tobacco and chewing gum. His brothers called him "the fighting grocer," which he hated. In his free time, he played soccer and road hockey.

Even though he wasn't fighting, the war was sometimes really hard work. Once, after his company arrived in Salonika, a town in northern Greece, he and some other soldiers were ordered to the ship's forward hold (a large storage room) to load supplies. They

(Here he is standing proudly in front of his plane.)

During an air raid, a bus hits and injures Lester. He's found unfit to fight because of his shattered nerves.

1918
Lester returns home to Canada.

World War I comes to an end.

In flight school, Lester's squadron commander thought the name Lester wasn't manly enough for a pilot, so he nicknamed him "Mike." It stuck. Mike liked the new moniker better than his given name. So, from this point forward, we'll refer to him as Mike.

worked all day. Then they worked on the docks, loading boats in the wind and rain until 4 a.m. They caught 15 minutes of sleep before the sergeant major got them back on their feet—wounded soldiers were coming in. Lester and company had to carry the wounded on their shoulders through mud, and set up a field hospital on straw over the mud in a gigantic, windy tent. They finally stopped to sleep after working for 48 hours straight.

Yet Lester still longed for combat, to be with his fellow Canadians in the trenches. He wasn't much use in the operating room. The sight of blood made him faint. His commanding officer kept him busy doing other things, but he was restless. Shell-shocked soldiers cried all night in pain, while Zeppelins (German blimps) floated overhead carrying bombs. Lester didn't feel as if his work was important enough to help win the war. And both his brothers were fighting soldiers, although Duke had been wounded. So he volunteered to fly fighter planes for the Royal Flying Corps in England.

He was trained as an officer cadet in Reading, England. Despite his busy training schedule, he still found time for sports. During a track-and-field day, he set a record for throwing a cricket ball a whopping 114 feet. It was such a big throw that the *London Times* even published his name.

Crashes and gashes

Ground training normally took a year, but the air force was so desperate for pilots at this point in the war that it was crammed into three weeks. His air training at Hendon, where he became "Mike," took even less time. After just two hours, the flight instructor shouted "Take off!" He had to fly by himself and had no time to be afraid—until it was time to land. Then he was scared. So scared he kept on flying until he was almost out of fuel. By then, he had to try to land…and he made it. But for the rest of his life, Mike would be sick to his stomach whenever he had to fly.

Although he didn't crash his first flight, he did soon after. His plane's engine died mid-flight and the plane landed hard. He was badly shaken and was given a couple of days off to rest. He and some friends decided to sneak off base to visit London and were sitting in a restaurant when the **air-raid siren** went off. Mike hopped on a bus to get back to his base, but a bomb exploded half a mile away. The scared driver stopped and ordered everyone off. Mike stepped onto the road in the blackout. He couldn't see a thing: there were no street lights, no car lights, not a single light anywhere. As he crossed Edgeware Road, he was hit by another bus and his leg was seriously gashed. His nerves were also shattered. For Mike, the war was over. About it all he said, "I got hurt before I got killed. You got to a point where you just went on until you were killed like all your friends were being killed."

Excused from active service, he was sent back to Canada while the air force decided what to do with him. Mike had developed a nervous disorder that was caused by two years of caring for mortally wounded men, then the plane crash and bus accident. In April 1918, Mike arrived in St. John, New Brunswick, 21 years old and two inches taller.

Given a couple of days off to rest, Mike heads to London. When an air-raid siren goes off, he hops on a bus to get back to his base, but a bomb explodes about half a mile away. The driver stops and orders everyone off.

1918

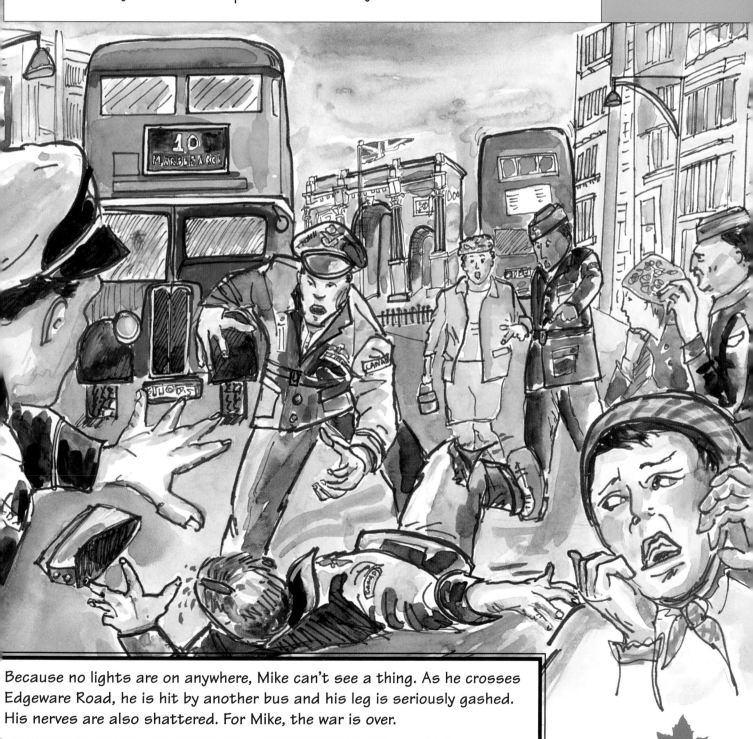

Because no lights are on anywhere, Mike can't see a thing. As he crosses Edgeware Road, he is hit by another bus and his leg is seriously gashed. His nerves are also shattered. For Mike, the war is over.

1919

Thinking he might like to be a lawyer, Mike tries working at a law firm, but quits within a week. Next, he plays baseball while on the payroll of a tire-and-rubber company. After that, he gets a job stuffing sausages at a meat-processing plant.

Reporting to work at 8 a.m., Mike is shown how to operate a compressed air tap. It forces sausage meat into a casing at high speed and under high pressure. Mike quickly learns to turn the tap off at the precise instant to avoid "dire consequences."

Chapter 3

Stuffing sausages

After Mike returned to Canada, he continued to serve his country by becoming an aerial navigation instructor in a Royal Air Force (RAF) school at the University of Toronto. Playing rugby helped calm his jangled nerves. He also went back to the University of Toronto, graduating with an honours degree in history in June 1919.

He still didn't have any idea what he wanted to do. He thought he might like being a lawyer and tried working at a law firm, but quit less than a week later. Next, he got a job at a tire-and-rubber company; after that, his uncle Edson got him a "glamorous" job stuffing sausages at the Fowler Packing Company in Hamilton. Then he went to Chicago to work at the Armour Fertilizer factory, where Uncle Edson was an executive. Years later, he joked that the Soviets claimed he'd once worked for an arms manufacturer.

In Chicago, Mike finally figured out what he wanted to do. He definitely didn't want to be a lawyer or a businessman—or to remain in Chicago. He wanted

1919
Mike graduates from the University of Toronto with an honours BA in history.

Mike's brother Duke arrives home safe, but his other brother, Vaughn, is emotionally damaged for life.

1920
Mike works in Chicago at the Armour Fertilizer plant.

1921
He moves to England to study at the Honours School of Modern History at Oxford University.

(Here he is playing hockey in Switzerland in 1922.)

1923
Mike takes a job as a lecturer of modern history at the University of Toronto.

1925
Mike marries Maryon Elspeth Moody.

1926
Maryon and Mike have a son named Geoffrey.

1929
They have a second child, a daughter named Patsy.

to become an academic, a professor in a university. He came back to Canada briefly before setting sail to study at the famous Oxford University in England. His family couldn't actually afford to send him to Oxford but he received a scholarship that helped pay for his education.

A Canadian in England

Founded around the 11th century, Oxford is one of the oldest and most formal universities in the world. Its famous "tutors" are teachers held in the greatest respect. There are even porters to help students carry their luggage. When Mike arrived on that first day, he was in awe of the ancient, ivy-covered buildings and he was delighted to spot a man who looked just like he imagined an Oxford porter would look. Mike asked him to help him with his bags. "Oh, yes, Pearson, we were expecting you," the man replied politely. "I'll show you to your room. But first let me introduce myself. I'm Powell, the senior tutor." Mike was totally embarrassed, but he got over it quickly.

He studied hard. He also wrote stories for the *Christian Guardian* newspaper back in Canada under the pen name "A Canadian in England." The paper paid him $10 for each story. Naturally, he got involved in plenty of sports as well. He played rugby, hockey, and lacrosse. He even became one of England's best lacrosse players and helped Oxford win the championship in 1922.

Herr Zigzag

Oxford had a very good hockey team too, and, of course, Mike was on it. When they travelled to Switzerland in 1922 for an exhibition game, the Swiss fans were so impressed by Mike's speed on the ice that they nicknamed him "Herr Zigzag."

Although he was only 26 , Mike's degree from Oxford landed him a job as a lecturer of **modern history** at the University of Toronto's Victoria College. He also coached university football, hockey, and lacrosse while playing squash and tennis. His amazing athletic ability earned him a spot in the Canadian National Tennis Championships.

As a history professor, Mike talked a lot to his students about World War I. What causes war? What could the world do to prevent wars from happening in the first place? How could we get all the nations of the world to work together for peace? Although he was only a young man, Mike was now thinking about the ideas that would one day make him an important leader in Canada and the world.

A surprised woman

Legend has it that one of Mike's fourth-year history students was particularly determined to get a good grade from him. So determined, in fact, that she got engaged to him. **Maryon Elspeth Moody** was only a few years

A medical board in London had prescribed rest for Mike's nervous disability but, back in Toronto, he returned to playing rugby. He found the physical exercise and the crowd's cheers a much better cure.

The causes of war

If you were born in Canada, it's likely that you've never experienced war. You may have seen it on your television screen, but that's far different from being there. Sadly, other Canadians know war all too well. They've come from places like Lebanon, Sri Lanka, Columbia, or Bosnia, all of which have suffered from brutal conflicts in recent years. But they too might find it difficult to explain what causes war—what makes thousands of people take up weapons and slaughter each other. The reason for every war is different, but often it comes from one of these problems:

- A government is trying to repress its people, or at least some of its people. In Sudan, for example, the national government has been hostile toward minorities who live in the border regions of that country, which has led to rebellions in at least two areas.

- A country or an ethnic group believes they should rule over an area that's held by another country. When Yugoslavia broke up in the 1990s, Croatians and Serbians fought over what their borders would be, and then both of them attacked Bosnia, trying to take land from that country.

- Some people want to impose their religious or social values on others, and decide the only way to do this is by force. This was the case with the Taliban, which took control of most of Afghanistan so that they could impose their own strict version of Islam on the people.

- Other wars have been caused by the personal ambitions of leaders who want to gain glory or power for themselves. Men like Alexander the Great, Napoleon, and Adolf Hitler have all believed they could conquer the world, and have all failed. On a smaller scale, the country of Somalia has been torn apart by petty warlords who care only about enriching themselves and controlling their own small territory.

These are simplified explanations for the causes of war, as they are often far more complex than can be explained in a few sentences. War often happens almost accidentally, when two sides, both of whom believing they're right, fail to come up with a compromise. A recent example of this is the war between Eritrea and Ethiopia. They were initially very friendly toward each other, but had a difference of opinion on where the border was between the two countries. The land in dispute was mostly uninhabited desert with a few small towns, but both sides believed that it belonged to them. In 1998, a few Eritrean soldiers were killed in this region, which prompted their government to send its army to occupy the territory. Ethiopia did the same, and soon a two-year-long war had begun. It would end only after 100,000 people had died and more than 500,000 more left homeless. The two sides signed a peace agreement in the year 2000, but tensions remain high and a return to war remains a strong possibility.

For more information about the causes of war, visit our website at www.jackfruitpress.com.

Mike never carried a wallet. He just wasn't interested in money. He'd stuff a few bills into his pocket—never enough—and always ended up borrowing a few bucks from his aides.

younger than Mike, an intelligent woman who spoke her own mind. A **feminist** long before it was fashionable, she planned to have her own career, but it never happened because she and Mike fell in love and were married on August 22, 1925.

On December 24, 1927, minutes before midnight, they welcomed their first child, Geoffrey, into the world. And you'll never guess what Mike's first decision as a father was. He talked the doctor into changing Geoffrey's birth certificate to say he was born on December 25. Mike figured he'd save money on presents by combining Geoffrey's birthday with Christmas.

Their daughter, Patsy, was born in March 1929. With two young children to raise, a home to run, and a husband who worked extremely long hours, Maryon soon realized that the exciting career she'd imagined wasn't going to happen. Like so many women of her time, she decided to be content with being Mrs. Pearson. Which doesn't mean she stopped speaking her own mind. Years after Mike had become prime minister, she spoke these famous words: "Behind every successful man is a surprised woman."

Maryon was a strong-minded woman like Mike's own mother. The only way Mike could devote so many hours to work was for Maryon to take over most of the household and family responsibilities. Sometimes she packed up the house and sold the car on her own when they had to move for Mike's job. She also looked after the money. Good thing, since Mike never even carried a wallet. Maryon paid all the bills and looked after their investments.

Everybody likes Mike

The Pearsons weren't rich but they were comfortable and very sensible. They didn't want to appear snobbish or wealthy so for many years they lived in an old house in the Sandy Hill area of Ottawa. Most of their friends lived in the suburb of Rockcliffe, a more upscale part of town.

When he was home, Mike was the first one up; he'd make the family breakfast—usually poached eggs, toast, and coffee. They had a cottage on the Gatineau River and a lot of friends. No matter where in the world they lived, the Pearsons were popular and were invited out constantly.

Just like when he was a boy, everyone liked Mike. He had a broad, warm smile that made people feel good. He loved laughing and jokes. And he laughed at himself most of all. Despite how outgoing he was in public, though, he was quiet and thoughtful in private.

Geoffrey and Patsy didn't see their dad much while they were growing up because he was away a lot of the time, especially when he became a diplomat. But they believed in the work he was doing. In a way, not having their dad around was like making a personal sacrifice to serve their country.

Like many other gifted intellectuals, Mike isn't much good at fixing things around the house. He admits that he can "change a light bulb correctly five times out of six."

On those rare occasions when Mike is home, he's always the first one up. He loves to make breakfast for the family. Usually all goes well, even when he gets help from the kids.

1931

As the Great Depression spreads, thousands lose their life savings and go bankrupt. Thirty per cent of people can't find a job anywhere. Families lose their homes. Some people have to line up in the street for a bowl of soup.

Mike is chosen to be the secretary of a government study on the effects of the Great Depression on wheat farming. He travels across the west, meeting farmers and seeing first-hand what a devastating effect the drought, dust storms, and depression have had on them and their livelihood.

Chapter 4

A diplomatic dude

By 1927, Canada was beginning to grow up. Although Canada had existed since **Confederation** in 1867, it was still a member of the **British Commonwealth**, a collection of countries that had once been British colonies. While many of these countries had gained some independence, Britain still maintained a great deal of control over them. This meant that Canada didn't have much of a voice in the world because most of its decisions were made for it back in England. Canada couldn't talk to other countries except through England, just like a parent speaking for a child.

1928
Mike (shown here on a fishing trip) joins the Department of External Affairs.

1929
On October 29, stock exchanges in New York, Toronto, Montreal, and other major cities around the world crash, triggering the Great Depression.

1931
Mike is secretary of a royal commission to study the effects of the depression on wheat farming.

1934
Mike is secretary of the Price Spreads Commission investigating businesses that are charging too much for their goods.

1935
Mike moves to England to work for Canada House.

1939
The German army invades Poland, and World War II begins.

Did you know?

"The Great Depression started with beans and ended with beans."

The stock market crash of '29 started when huge crops of beans glutted the markets, driving down coffee prices.

Stocks like Folgers and Maxwell House lost their value on the US stock market. Then, like a rolling avalanche, other overpriced company shares lost their value too.

Stocks that were worth millions suddenly weren't worth the paper they were printed on. In the space of a few days, the stock-market crash sparked a slide into international poverty that would become known as the Great Depression.

Rural families in the west were driven off their farms by years of drought. The city poor had no control over what had happened; all these hungry people knew was that just a plate of beans would keep them alive.

But Canada had begun taking steps toward independence. A new government department, External Affairs, had been created in 1909 to deal with international relations and Canadian diplomats abroad. External Affairs was run by the prime minister himself, helped by an undersecretary. It was this man who persuaded Mike to take the entrance exam in 1928. Because Mike scored highest of all the contestants across Canada, he got the job. At the time, there were only 14 people in the department.

Black Thursday

Now he worked for the government as a **civil servant**, writing reports and giving speeches. But, only a year later, the stock-market crash of 1929 shattered the world. It started with "**Black Thursday**" at the New York Stock Exchange, when too many people, worried about falling stock prices, sold too many all at once. The selling frenzy quickly spread to stock exchanges around the world, including Toronto and Montreal. Black Monday was even worse and, by Black Tuesday, people were panicking. They went from rich to poor overnight. Stocks that were worth millions suddenly weren't worth the paper they were printed on. In the space of a few days, the stock-market crash sparked an entire decade of struggle that would become known as the **Great Depression**.

People lost their life savings and whole companies went bankrupt. Thirty per cent of Canada's workforce couldn't find a job anywhere. Families lost their homes. Some even lined up in the street for a bowl of soup. The shame of being penniless caused many people to suffer extreme stress.

The government realized it had to take a leadership role in putting Canada back on its feet. In 1931, it created a **royal commission** to study the effects of the Great Depression on the grain industry. Mike Pearson was picked to be secretary of the study. Although he'd always been a hard worker, Mike pushed himself even more than usual. He would go to work at 9 a.m. and stay until midnight, sometimes on weekends as well.

Hey, Pearson! Here's your OBE!

In recognition of his devoted service to the country, Prime Minister R. B. Bennett recommended Mike for a special award, the **Order of the British Empire**, or OBE. This was a great honour, but because Mike was away, he couldn't receive his award in a big ceremony. Instead, one day when he was playing tennis, a car pulled up to the court. One of Mike's friends from the **governor general**'s office hopped out of the car and tossed him a small box over the fence. "Here's your OBE!" he said.

During this period, the government often sent Mike to discuss important matters with other countries. He went to naval conferences in London,

The League of Nations and the United Nations

One of the important lessons of World War I was that nations needed a way to resolve disputes using international law instead of their armies. It was decided that a worldwide organization, known as the League of Nations, would be created to mediate between countries and prevent the outbreak of another world war.

The league started in 1919, but soon found that it was difficult to maintain peace around the world. The league's main problem was that it had no armed forces to control its member states. Unable to stop the violent behaviour of countries like Nazi Germany, the League of Nations finally collapsed with the outbreak of World War II. It had failed to achieve its primary purpose: to avoid another world war.

Men like Mike Pearson had not given up on the idea of an international body that could prevent wars and deal with other global problems. While Pearson was working as a diplomat in the United States during the 1940s, he became heavily involved in the planning of this new organization. His work helped to bring about the United Nations in 1945.

The UN was designed to be more effective than the League of Nations. Nearly every nation in the world was part of it, and the most powerful countries (China, France, Great Britain, the Soviet Union, and the United States) were given more influence. The UN Security Council was created to make binding decisions and impose them with military force. Peacekeepers, the UN military forces—an idea put forward by Mike Pearson—have been used all over the world to help stop wars and preserve the peace.

Canadians have sent over 100,000 soldiers to serve in dozens of peacekeeping missions around the world, which are often very dangerous. For example, in 1993, Canadian and French peacekeepers had a fierce battle with hundreds of Croatian troops during an operation in Yugoslavia. The battle of Medak Pocket, also called "Canada's secret battle," ended when the Croatians withdrew. They'd suffered 27 casualties; several UN peacekeepers were wounded. Their intervention was too late to stop the ethnic cleansing (torture and mass murder of civilians) in the area. Fortunately, the peacekeepers arrived in time to gather evidence of the atrocities that had been committed.

The cost of these missions has been high—so far, more than 100 Canadians have been killed while serving as peacekeepers around the world. Despite this, most Canadians are proud of the peacekeeping work our soldiers have done and believe that we should continue to serve in UN operations.

For more information about the United Nations, visit our website at www.jackfruitpress.com.

At the coronation of King George VI, Mike, who was serving as an usher, was told to stand behind a huge column in Westminster Abbey. He couldn't see the ceremony there, so he and another usher climbed way up a spiral staircase until they found an opening large enough to let them see it.

Did they get in trouble? No one knows.

League of Nations sessions in Belgium, and conferences in Geneva. All were about world disarmament. Everywhere he went he made friends. People were impressed by his diplomatic skills, his hard work, and his easygoing, country-boy manner. People felt at home with him and trusted him. And he had a real gift for resolving conflict. He recognized that successful compromise meant that no one should be humiliated.

In 1935, with only two days' notice, he was sent to London to work for Canada House, the Canadian government's office in England. His old teacher from university, **Vincent Massey**, was Canada's high commissioner to England and his new boss. Small world!

In London, Mike met **Winston Churchill**, who would later become prime minister of England, and he got to be an usher at the coronation of **King George VI** in Westminster Abbey.

The war to end all wars, part two

Mike returned to Canada for a summer vacation in 1939, four years after he'd moved to London. Despite how much he was looking forward to a relaxing holiday, he felt a sense of gloom. He was worried that another world war was about to start. Winston Churchill had already warned people about a war in a speech two years before. Even once he was back home in Canada, Mike couldn't shake his sense that bad things were coming. Germany's leader, **Adolf Hitler**, had been building up his supply of weapons and had begun to take back land that Germany had lost after World War I. This was shocking for many politicians, diplomats, and national leaders. Hitler had convinced them he was the peace-loving head of a Germany that was civilized and sophisticated, a land of classical music and fine literature.

But Mike had not been fooled. He was in the minority along with a few people like Churchill. Hard as it is for us to imagine today, many people didn't think this little German chancellor was anyone worth paying attention to. No one suspected the atrocities Hitler would commit against millions of innocent people.

Prime Minister King had met with Hitler shortly before and had also been fooled. He'd walked away from his meeting with Hitler thinking that Germany would not risk going to war. Mike told him the opposite. He insisted that Hitler would go to war at any moment. King didn't believe him. But Mike felt such urgency to get back to England that he didn't travel by ship, which was the usual way at that time. Instead, he flew across the Atlantic to get there faster. Passenger planes were brand new and Mike became the first Canadian official to fly across the Atlantic. A few days after he arrived back at Canada House, Germany invaded Poland and **World War II** began.

In Germany, Adolf Hitler is preparing for war while insisting that he is a peace-loving leader. But Mike is one of the few who hasn't been fooled. He cuts his Canadian holiday short to hurry back to England.

As much as he hates flying, Mike insists on rushing back by plane because he feels such a sense of urgency. Only days after he arrives back in London, Germany invades Poland and World War II begins.

As the war rages on, children are evacuated to the countryside. Food is scarce and rationed. Rumours of Nazi death camps are spreading. Many people fear Germany might take over the world.

BBC

On both sides of the Atlantic, a major challenge is keeping the public's spiri up. Mike does his best to help. From London, he broadcasts radio reports t Canada on a regular basis. With TV not yet invented, radio is the most immediate source of information about what's happening on the war front.

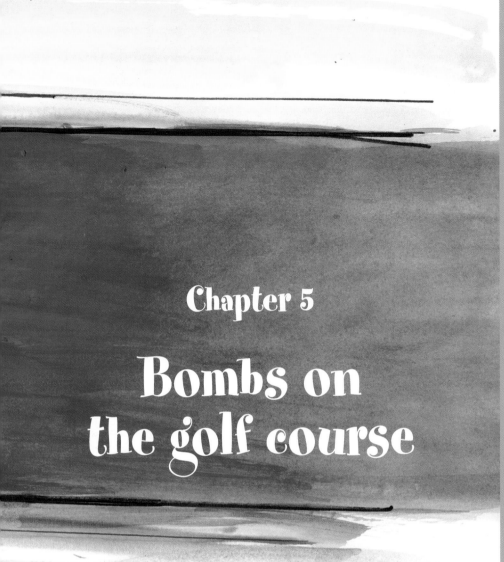

Chapter 5

Bombs on the golf course

The two world wars were very different for Canada, and for Mike too. In World War I, he'd been a young soldier serving his country. Now, as a senior member of External Affairs, his job was to decide how Canada would declare war on Germany. In World War I, the British government had decided that Canada should join the fight, but this time, Canada, through an act of Parliament, had the power to make up its own mind.

Because he was assistant high commissioner at Canada House, Mike was asked to write up Canada's declaration of war. He talked to some experts, wrote a sample letter and sent it to the King of England for his comments. Everyone liked the wording of the letter and a formal copy was sent to Ottawa. It was passed in Parliament and signed by Prime Minister King. Canada was now officially at war with Germany.

The Corky Affair

Mike's next challenge was furry and had four legs. Some Canadian soldiers had arrived in England with their battalion mascot, a dog named Corky. But British law said that all animals from other countries had to be quarantined (kept isolated) for three months. The soldiers protested that they'd be too homesick without their dog. Mike felt sorry for them but there was nothing he could do. The soldiers were determined not to abandon Corky, though, and came up with a plan. They bought another dog that looked just like him, and two handsome soldiers were sent on a mission to make friends with the two pretty girls who ran the dog pound. They convinced the girls to switch dogs, and Corky returned to his regiment.

World War II was a tough time for everyone. Almost every Canadian had a father, son, brother, or uncle who was away fighting. And almost everyone had already lost loved ones in World War I, which they'd thought was "the war to end all wars." In Britain and Europe, people lived under bombing sieges and children were evacuated to the British countryside for safety. Some kids were even sent to Canada. Food was rationed because it was scarce. Rumours that the **Nazis** were "deporting" Jewish people were spreading. Many people feared that the Nazis might take over the world. On both sides of the Atlantic, one of the hardest jobs was keeping the public's spirits up. Mike did his best to help from London. He broadcast radio reports to Canada during the war. With no TV yet, radio was the most immediate source of information about what was happening in the rest of the world.

Life during wartime

Bombs were falling on London. When the air-raid sirens sounded, Mike and his staff at Canada House would go to the basement for safety and stay there until the all-clear was given by a special telephone. One day, the special phone didn't ring and they stayed in the basement for hours, hot and sweating, not knowing if they should be scared or not. Mike volunteered to go upstairs and see. Everything was fine. It was a lovely, sunny day. It had been a false alarm and someone had forgotten to call them.

Mike hardly slept during this time in London. He read the war reports and the telegrams, and knew just how badly the war was going. He knew that Britain was being defended by a few thousand young Royal Air Force pilots flying fighter planes against bombers, and by what was left of the British army, the royal navy, and the First Canadian Division of the army stationed in England.

A famous speech that Prime Minister Churchill gave promised that Britons would never surrender, but fight in the streets if they had to. This courageous statement cheered and inspired the British. It also told Mike he need not fear that Britain would surrender as France had done.

Soon after, Mike was transferred back to Ottawa as chief assistant to the deputy minister of external affairs. He never forgot the bravery of the

Mike used a pseudonym when broadcasting on wireless radio. He called himself Michael Macdonald. He reported on air raids, the air battles of the RAF, and Canadian visitors' safe arrivals at English ports.

British people, who had the guts to carry on with regular life—paperboys still delivered papers and milkmen still delivered milk—in the middle of bombs dropping and fires burning. They'd even managed to get in their golf. Once, during a game, Mike's caddy told him to aim his shot so that his ball wouldn't hit an unexploded bomb that lay on the fairway.

Bombs are falling all over London. When the air-raid sirens blare, Mike and his staff at Canada House rush to the basement for safety and stay there until the all-clear is given.

1941

One day, the special phone doesn't ring. Mike and his staff wait in the basement for hours, hot and sweating, not knowing what's happened. Mike volunteers to go upstairs and see. Everything is fine. It's a lovely, sunny day. It had been a false alarm but someone forgot to tell them.

While in Washington, Mike helps to establish the United Nations and some of its agencies. Having suggested that the UN do something about world hunger, he is elected chairman of a newly created commission to deal with it.

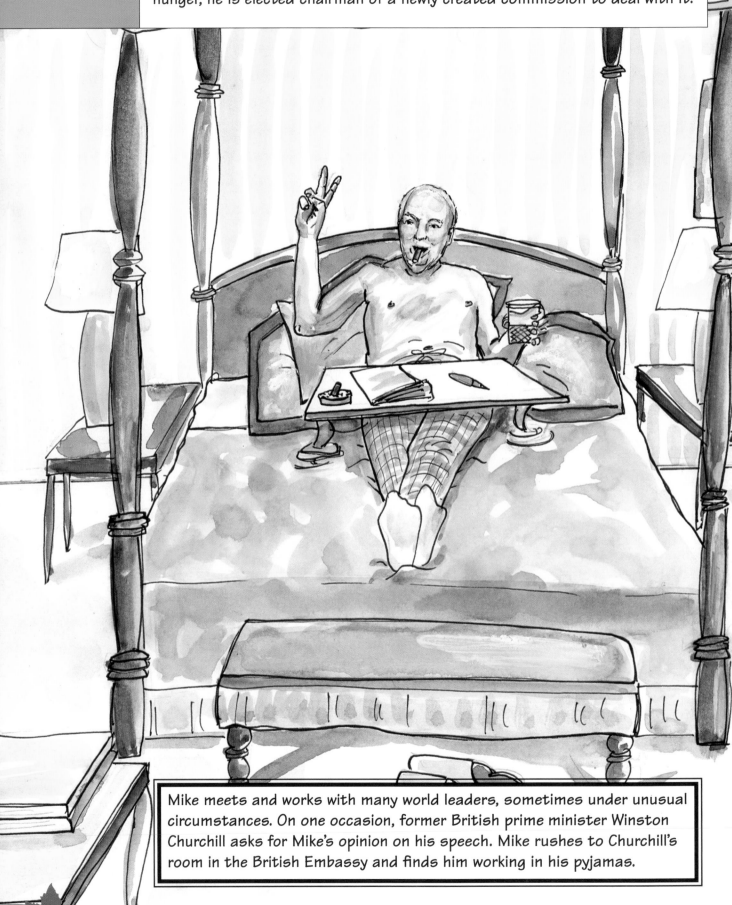

Mike meets and works with many world leaders, sometimes under unusual circumstances. On one occasion, former British prime minister Winston Churchill asks for Mike's opinion on his speech. Mike rushes to Churchill's room in the British Embassy and finds him working in his pyjamas.

Chapter 6

Top secret and top of the world

Mike's next job, which he began in June 1942, was working for the Canadian Embassy in Washington. He would stay there for four years, moving up from ministerial positions to become the **ambassador** for Canada in 1945. While he was ambassador, his family lived on the second and third floors of the embassy, in the biggest apartment they'd ever seen.

As always, Mike made new friends and attended many social functions. One year, his daughter begged to be taken along to a birthday party for President **Franklin D. Roosevelt**. Patsy was so excited about meeting movie stars in the receiving line that she went through twice. She was thrilled when the famous actor, James Cagney, said, "Haven't I seen you before, little girl?"

Mike also found time for sports. He helped organize baseball games between the Canadian Embassy and the US State Department. It was lots of fun for Mike and his team even though they went out of their way to avoid winning every time. As Mike later playfully explained, they did this to avoid creating an international crisis!

1942
Mike starts work at the Canadian Legation in Washington, DC.

1943
Mike is elected chair of Food and Agriculture Organization.

1945
World War II ends.

Mike becomes the Canadian ambassador to the United States.

1946
Mike and his family move back to Ottawa, where he becomes deputy minister of external affairs.

1947-49
Mike and other Canadians help form the North Atlantic Treaty Organization (NATO).

1948
Mike joins the Liberal party. He's elected to the House of Commons.

He's appointed secretary of state for the Department of External Affairs.

1952-53
Mike serves as president of the United Nations General Assembly.

1956
Egypt and Great Britain, France, and Israel fight for control of the Suez Canal.

Mike proposes the creation of a UN peacekeeping force.

1957
Mike wins the Nobel Peace Prize for his efforts in ending the Suez War.

During his time in Washington, Mike participated in the conferences that established the United Nations and such powerful agencies as the UN Food and Agricultural Organization (FAO). The US government wanted to coordinate international efforts to end world hunger. To do this, the UN set up a commission and elected Mike as chairman. He made speeches and met with many world leaders, sometimes under unusual circumstances. Once, when Winston Churchill was in Washington and asked for his help with a speech, Mike rushed to Churchill's room in the British Embassy and found him still in his pajamas. That didn't stop him from making corrections to the speech Churchill was working on that day— a speech that would become famous for using the term "Iron Curtain" to describe the boundary between Western Europe and the Soviet-bloc countries of Eastern Europe.

Secret missions

Mike's skills as a trusted diplomat were legendary. One time during the war, when the British Foreign Office heard he was travelling from London to Canada with a stop in New York, they trusted him to deliver a top-secret document to the US headquarters of British security. Mike kept absolute secrecy about his mission and even slept with the document under his pillow. At the appointed day and time, he delivered it to an office in New York City. He never found out what the contents of the envelope were.

Another time, he was sent to a top-secret meeting at the **Pentagon**. He told everyone that he was going to a meeting in New York, but actually went to Washington. When he arrived at the Pentagon, he snuck in through a back door. He then walked through the kitchens to the secret meeting room where he talked with the Americans and the British about the current European situation. People trusted Mike and he didn't let them down.

Mike becomes a minister

In the fall of 1946, the Pearsons moved back to Ottawa and Mike became deputy minister of external affairs. After two years on the job, he was asked by Prime Minister **Louis St. Laurent** to be secretary of state for the Department of External Affairs. This was a position that St. Laurent had held until succeeding King as prime minister. To qualify for the job, Mike first had to be an elected politician. Before doing that, he had to join the Liberal party. He ran in the next election and won a seat in the Algoma East riding (in northern Ontario, 20,000 square miles in size).

The next years were incredibly productive for Mike. He drafted a speech in which Canada proposed the **North Atlantic Treaty Organization (NATO)** and acted as chairman of the NATO council during the 1951–52 session. He also headed the Canadian delegation to the UN from 1945 to 1956. As chairman of the UN's Special Committee on Palestine in 1947,

Mike once confided to a colleague that he could advise and make lists for the Americans but, when important decisions were to be made, he was always asked to leave the meeting. Mike was smart enough to know he had little power in helping to set US policy.

Mike's skills as a trusted diplomat are legendary. Important people trust Mike with top-secret missions, and he never lets them down.

Mike is sent to a meeting at the Pentagon in Washington, but tells everyone he's going to a meeting in New York. Arriving at the Pentagon, he sneaks in through a back door. He then walks through the kitchen to a secret room, where he meets with the Americans and the British.

Did you know?

In 1960, Maryon and Patsy Pearson joined the Voice of Women to protest the growing climate of belief in nuclear weapons, and the stockpiling in great numbers of these warheads by the USSR and the United States. Maryon said that, as women, they saw the utter stupidity of male dependence on such weapons.

Mike became the first Canadian to win the Nobel Prize for peace. Because of him, Canada gained the reputation of being a peace-loving nation.

Mike laid the groundwork for the creation of the state of Israel. And, in 1952, in addition to all of his other duties as an MP, he became president of the United Nations General Assembly.

The threat of war

One of Mike's biggest challenges came in 1956. Egypt was fuming mad at the United States and Great Britain for withdrawing their financial support for a huge dam project. Egypt's president, **Gamal Abdel Nasser**, was so angry that he seized control of the Suez Canal, a major shipping route that was protected by an international treaty. This treaty had guaranteed that the canal would remain open to all international traffic. Egypt's action angered Britain and France, so, together with Israel, they waged a war—known as the **Suez War**—to take back the canal from Nasser.

The United States asked the United Nations to give an order to stop the fighting, but Mike didn't think that would work. The nations were fighting for what they believed in and nobody wanted to be the one to give in. Instead, he came up with an idea for a special military force that would work for the UN rather than for any one country. He flew to the UN headquarters in New York with his ideas written on little scraps of paper. The minute he arrived, he was mobbed by UN delegates all curious to hear his proposal. They overwhelmingly approved Mike's plan for a peacekeeping force. Canadian troops participated in the new peacekeeping force while the invading nations withdrew from the Suez.

Nobel Prize winner

A war had been prevented and Mike Pearson was now an international hero. A year later, the phone in his office rang. It was a news reporter calling to ask if Mike had anything to announce. Mike was confused. He didn't realize that he'd just won the Nobel Peace Prize. When the reporter assured him it was true, the only word Mike could get out of his mouth was "Gosh!"

Of Mike's years as Canada's minister of external affairs, author Gordon Donaldson wrote, "Mike became the best known and most admired Canadian in the world" and "the scrubbed and hopeful face of Mike Pearson was the face of Canada."

Mike's easygoing style changed the face of international diplomacy. He was an all-round good guy without stuffy pride—a gentle, cheerful fellow who saw no point in humiliating a person or a country. The way he saw it, any settlement was better than war. Mike had a big advantage: he loved his work as a diplomat, and enjoyed living at the edge of world politics.

It was when he entered the arena of Canadian politics that his shining image started to dull.

The Nobel Prize

Alfred Nobel was a Swedish chemist who, in 1866, invented dynamite. Dynamite was a powerful explosive, and Nobel believed it would be a valuable tool for mining and construction uses. It was indeed useful, but mostly for war, as armies used it to destroy their enemies and cause massive destruction. When Alfred's brother, Ludvig, died in 1888, a French newspaper mistakenly ran an obituary for Alfred, condemning his invention and calling him a "merchant of death." After reading this, Alfred decided he wanted to leave a better legacy of his life. In his will, he left nearly all of his money toward the creation of the Nobel prizes—to honour those who make a significant contribution to society. These awards are given out every year in the areas of physics, chemistry, medicine, economics, literature—and, of course, peace.

The Nobel Peace Prize is given to people or organizations who "have done the most or the best work for fraternity between the nations, for the abolition or reduction of standing armies, and for the holding and promotion of peace congresses." It was first awarded in 1901, and recipients have included Martin Luther King Jr., Mother Teresa, and Nelson Mandela. In some cases, the award has gone to groups or organizations. In 1997, the winner was the International Campaign to Ban Landmines, which was a worldwide effort that included many Canadians. These were just ordinary people who managed to work together and convince their governments that it was wrong to use land mines because of the damage and death they cause to civilians.

Mike Pearson is the only individual Canadian to win the Noble Peace Prize, which he earned for his work in ending the Suez War of 1956. It was his idea to create, in his words, "a truly international peace and police force," that would become known as United Nations peacekeepers. "I regret the use of military force," Pearson told a UN meeting, but added "we need action, not only to end the fighting, but to make the peace." He was right about this; since then, peacekeepers have been used to stop conflicts around the world. In 1988, the Nobel prize was awarded to all those who served as United Nations peacekeepers.

An Egyptian family leaves their bombed-out home during the Suez War.

For more information about the Nobel prizes, visit our website at www.jackfruitpress.com.

1963

John Diefenbaker gets all the attention. His wild claims get turned into headlines and radio and television sound bites. By contrast, Mike is quiet, reasonable, and logical—not nearly as exciting or dramatic.

Mike likes being prime minister, but all the quarrelling and arguing drives him up the wall. In spite of his diplomatic skills, he's often angered by his old rival and ends up saying things he later regrets. He even loses friends.

Chapter 7

Great honour, terrible job

Had Mike stayed on as president of the UN General Assembly, he probably would have become secretary general and fulfilled his dream of serving all the nations. Another adventure was waiting for him, though. Back in Canada, Prime Minister Louis St. Laurent was retiring and Mike was the man chosen to replace him as leader of the **Liberal party**. Mike ran for the job out of a sense of duty to his own country.

Even though he'd become a hero on the world stage, Mike soon found out that his reputation at home was in trouble. Conservative critics were doing their best to try to tarnish Mike's peacekeeping victory in the eyes of average Canadians. Progressive Conservative leader **John Diefenbaker** led the attack, blaming Mike for letting Britain down by not allowing it to go to war to protect its interests in the Suez Canal. Another minister said that Mike had "knifed Canada's best friends [Britain and France] in the back." In truth, Britain and France were glad that a war had been prevented.

The battle of Mike and Dief

The 1963 election campaign highlighted the widely different personalities of the two leaders. Diefenbaker loved politics and enjoyed fighting in public. Mike didn't. Diefenbaker led the way with loud accusations that were easily turned into newspaper headlines. His wild claims made for great radio and television sound bites too. Diefenbaker came across as a

Results of the 1963 election:

Lester B. Pearson becomes
Canada's 14th prime minister

Population:	18,238,247
Eligible voters:	9,910,757
Valid votes cast:	7,958,636

How the numbers stacked up:

Party	# votes	# seats
Liberal	3,293,790	129
PC	2,591,614	95
NDP	1,037,857	17
SoCred	940,703	24
Other	30,112	0
Total	7,894,076	265

Key issue: allowing nuclear weapons
on Canadian soil

Did you know?

As prime minister, Mike came up with a fairer way to select people who'd applied to come to Canada. His way was to scrap laws based on race, colour, or religion and give points for age, education, skills, employment opportunities in Canada, and degree of fluency in English or French. Higher scores made a person a more suitable choice for immigrating to Canada.

man who really knew what he was talking about. By contrast, Mike was quiet, reasonable, and logical—not nearly as exciting or dramatic. Diefenbaker's Conservatives won by a landslide. In Opposition, Mike had five years in which to rebuild the Liberal party.

In the election of 1963, Mike became Canada's 14th prime minister when his party won the election with a **minority government**. He would have to use all of his diplomatic skills to get a majority of MPs in Parliament to agree on his policies. Mike and his government made mistakes. He was often angered by his old rival, Diefenbaker, and said things he later regretted. He even lost friends. Although he liked being prime minister and working for his country, all the quarrelling and arguing drove him up the wall.

In 1965, Mike decided to ask Canadians for a majority government and called another election. He said that if the Liberals didn't win a majority, he'd resign. The Liberals won but were still two seats short of a majority. Mike tried to resign the next day but his cabinet ministers convinced him to stay on as leader.

One of these ministers, **Judy LaMarsh**, made her mark in Canadian history by championing the cause of women and establishing the Royal Commission on the Status of Women in Canada. Women from across the country appeared before this commission to voice their opinions and serve as witnesses to the discrimination they experienced.

His government had the support of the **Social Credit** and **New Democratic** parties during this second term, and he still had lots of ideas for new policies and programs. He brought in new legislation to deal more fairly with immigration applicants. So that new Canadians would feel welcome, he removed the racial exclusions of the past. A new law promoted a **points system** through which people of other nations could qualify to enter Canada by having enough points given for age, education, skills, employment opportunities in Canada, and degree of fluency in English or French.

Other legislation helped to make Canada the kinder, gentler nation it is today: a pension plan for people over 65, free medical care, government loans for college and university students, and money for rural development. He also signed the Canada–United States Auto Pact, which helped bring high-paying jobs to Canada.

The importance of language

One of the big worries Mike had to deal with was Quebec. Many French-speaking Quebecers thought that Quebec was a "nation," with its own distinct language and culture. Some of them thought Quebec should have special powers that the other provinces didn't need. Others were separatists—people who wanted Quebec to separate from Canada and become an independent country.

Mike hopes a new flag will bring Canada together. He invites everyone in Canada to design one. Over 2,000 designs are submitted. Some are funny, others just strange.

1964

In the end, three flag designs are chosen. The House of Commons debates them for an entire summer. Eventually, the government invokes closure (a rule to stop debate). At 2 a.m. on December 15, 1964, Canada's new flag is adopted. It is raised for the first time two months later, on February 15, 1965.

Mike drew on all of his diplomatic listening skills. He wondered how to make French-speaking Canadians feel they belonged in Canada, how to create peace in the country he loved. He wished that he spoke better French and thought about the importance of language, the importance of being understood and valued. To try to answer some of these concerns, he set up the Royal Commission on Bilingualism and Biculturalism, which led to a bilingual civil service. And he appointed more francophone cabinet ministers. He dreamed of the day when every person in Canada's public service could speak both languages well.

This was typical of how Mike worked. He spent an enormous amount of time listening, not only to Quebec but to all the provinces so he could hear the concerns of all Canadians. "Our country's existence," he said, "has always depended upon achieving unity of human purpose within the diversity of our linguistic and social backgrounds."

The Maple Leaf

Part of his plan to achieve unity in Canada was to create a uniquely Canadian flag. Until now, the **Red Ensign** had been Canada's flag. It featured the **Union Jack** and the Canadian **coat of arms**. Many Canadians, especially war veterans, were loyal to the Red Ensign because it had represented Canada around the world. But it also associated Canada with Britain, and Mike wanted to change that. He hoped a new flag would bring the country together. And he wanted it done in time for Canada's 100th birthday in 1967.

It wasn't easy. A lot of war veterans were against a new flag and so was Diefenbaker. He and Mike argued endlessly and, at one point, even stopped talking to each other. To cool the issue, Pearson announced that all Canadians could help design the flag. The government received over 2,000 designs. Some were pretty funny: a group of university students sent in a drawing of nine beavers peeing on a frog; from Regina came an electric flag, complete with flashing lights.

In the end, three designs were chosen: a version of the original Red Ensign with a French *fleur-de-lys* and a smaller Union Jack in the corner; a flag that contained three maple leaves; and a third drawing that came in at the last minute, a single red maple leaf on a white background edged by two red bars. The three flags then went to the **House of Commons** for debate. The debate lasted the entire summer.

Eventually, the government called closure, a rule that can stop a debate that goes on too long. At 2 a.m. on December 15, 1964, Canada's new flag was passed by Parliament. It was raised for the first time exactly two months later, on February 15, 1965.

Cabinet Minister Judy LaMarsh, Mike's wife Maryon, and many women's groups made Mike more aware of the discrimination that women were experiencing in all walks of life.

One group leader threatened that a million women would march on Parliament Hill if Mike didn't take action. Mike responded by setting up a royal commission to look into the whole issue.

Canada's part in the Vietnam War

Mike's successor, Pierre Elliott Trudeau, said that Canada being next to the United States is "like sleeping with an elephant; no matter how friendly and even-tempered is the beast, one is affected by every twitch and grunt." One example of how true this is comes from Canada's experience during the Vietnam War. Although Canada remained officially neutral in this conflict between the United States and North Vietnam, Canadians did play a significant role.

After Vietnam ousted its French masters in 1954, the country was divided into two states: North Vietnam, which was a communist country, and South Vietnam, which was ruled by dictators and generals but friendly toward the United States and other Western nations. The United States gave a lot of support to the South Vietnamese government, believing that if this country fell to the communists, it would start a chain reaction that would lead to the rest of Asia also becoming communist. Meanwhile, the North Vietnamese— and many people in the south—believed that they were fighting to liberate their country from foreign governments, so they decided to join with the communists and fight against the South Vietnamese government.

During the 1960s, the United States became more and more involved in this civil war and, from 1965 to 1973, hundreds of thousands of US troops were sent to fight in the jungles of Vietnam. The Americans, who had better weapons and training, won many battles against the communists, but they could never destroy them. Meanwhile, massacres and atrocities were committed by both sides, and thousands of soldiers were getting killed.

Support for the war among the American people plummeted, and in the early 1970s the United States slowly withdrew its forces. By 1975, the communists conquered the entire country, ending a war that had cost the lives of between one and two million Vietnamese people and nearly 60,000 US soldiers.

While the United States became more involved in the war, Pearson and his government believed that the best course would be to seek peace and use diplomacy, but they also supported the US efforts. Canada supported South Vietnam by contributing $29 million to its war effort against the north. Canadians even did some spying on behalf of the Americans. Furthermore, 10,000 Canadians joined the US army to fight in Vietnam, and many businesses in Canada became wealthy by selling supplies (such as food, boots, and berets), materials (such as metal for armour, wiring, and shell casings) and weapons to the US military.

Meanwhile, tens of thousands of Americans fled to Canada during this time. Called draft dodgers and army deserters, they were men who either refused to join the US army or left after being enlisted. These people were against the war, and received support from anti-war activists in Canada. Even after the war ended, most of these Americans remained in Canada because they were so opposed to their government's war-like stance.

Canada's participation in the Vietnam War raises some interesting questions. For one, how did the government, whose leader (Mike) was renowned as a peacekeeper, get so involved in this war? Also, since a large portion of Canadians were opposed to the war, what motivated Canadian companies to get involved?

For more information about the Vietnam War, visit our website at www.jackfruitpress.com.

In 1966, Canada was gripped by its very own spy scandal!

From 1958 to 1961, Gerda Munsinger, an alleged East German spy, had been involved with several members of John Diefenbaker's cabinet, including the associate minister of defence.

Five years later, when the news went public, it caused an uproar. People wondered if national security had been put at risk.

To squelch the scandal, Mike created a commission to investigate it. Then, to get folks thinking about other things, he started a new debate on capital punishment in the House of Commons.

Time to move on

During this time, Mike was deeply unhappy that the United States was at war with Vietnam. He gave a speech in Philadelphia suggesting that the United States stop bombing in North Vietnam and think about a peaceful solution to the conflict. Mike believed in telling the truth, even if it was hard to hear.

He told his government colleagues to do the same. Desperate to shift attention away from a spy scandal, Mike introduced debate on the death penalty. He proposed outlawing capital punishment for all crimes except the murder of police officers or prison guards. Although he lost the first vote, a year later capital punishment was abolished for a trial period of five years and was later permanently outlawed in Canada in 1976.

By 1967, Mike was 70, and tired. Even his friends were telling him it was time to move on. Besides, after all these years, he still didn't like politics much. He'd faced the depressing rants of his opponents for too long.

It was also Canada's centennial, the 100th anniversary of Confederation. A whole year of festivities took place, including the joyous **Expo '67**. On December 14, when the parties were almost over, Mike announced his retirement from politics. He thought it would be best for Canada if a French-speaking Quebecer succeeded him, so he backed **Pierre Elliott Trudeau**, who would become Canada's next prime minister.

Mike and Maryon retired in Ottawa and he went back to academic life. He became chancellor of Carleton University, where he lectured on history and political science. He also began writing his memoirs. When the first volume came out in 1972, it went straight to the top of the best-seller lists. He went on book tours and talked about the good old days.

His one regret was that his children had grown up too fast and that his career had not allowed more time with them when they were children. In later years, he enjoyed the time spent with his grandchildren and his new dog, Toby.

But illness struck. In 1972, the cancer he had been battling for several years finally spread. Mike died on December 27, 1972, with his children and Maryon near him. He was 75 years old. His burial place is MacLaren Cemetery in Wakefield, Quebec. Wakefield is in the Gatineau region near Ottawa, a place he'd spent many happy holidays with family and friends.

Mike believes in telling the truth, even when it's hard to hear. On a trip to Philadelphia, he publicly criticizes the United States for bombing North Vietnam. This angers President Johnson; Mike has attacked US policy on US soil.

I'm really tired of getting advice from #!* ignorant, know-nothing do-gooders like you!

I want peace too. I wish we could get out of Vietnam, but we can't let those communists take over!

But your air-bombing campaign isn't working! Let North Vietnam come up with a position you could negotiate.

Invited to visit President Johnson's Texas ranch, Mike thinks he's taking part in a diplomatic event. He shows up dressed in a traditional three-piece suit. Johnson meets him in a cowboy outfit and takes him for a ride around his ranch, secret-service men in tow. Mike listens politely as the president berates him for publicly taking a stand against the way United States is conducting the war.

(This image combines two separate events.)

War is not an option . . .

"No country in the world is more envied, and with such good reason, as Canada.

"No country has a greater destiny ahead if we wish to make it so."

*Lester B. Pearson
1968*

While there's no doubt that Mike Pearson was a brilliant statesman, his diplomatic skills did not always serve him well in politics. His sincere efforts to listen to everyone and to try to accommodate all views were often misinterpreted as signs of poor leadership and lack of direction. And although he was a great thinker with wonderful ideas to share with Canada and the world, his funny voice and lisp made it hard for people to listen to his speeches. When he had larger issues on his mind, Mike tended to ignore other challenges that were less important to him. For instance, although he was a dedicated believer in human rights, his critics feel that he neglected to advocate for the rights of women in the workplace.

He was in power for only five years, but Mike's achievements as PM are outstanding. Just look at them: a distinct Canadian flag, the Canada Pension Plan for seniors, universal free medicare, and a fairer immigration policy that helped new Canadians to feel welcome here.

There's more. Government help for college and university students, money for rural development, the Royal Commission on Bilingualism and Biculturalism, a bilingual civil service . . . and, finally, the Royal Commission on the Status of Women in Canada, which shone a light on discrimination against women. It was fitting that the centennial celebrations of 1967 mirrored the great optimism that Canadians felt during the later years of his government.

Any settlement is better

Mike knew people well, and had a great talent for recognizing ability in his colleagues. Three future prime ministers were members of his 1965 cabinet: Pierre Trudeau, John Turner, and Jean Chrétien. When quizzed about his success, Mike said he did it all "by hard work and long hours; by (being) . . . available for whatever was to be done; by welcoming every opportunity for new and more responsible duties; and by accumulating all the experience possible in all the varied aspects of my profession."

Having travelled abroad extensively, Mike was known by many world leaders. He was trusted because he was an idea man who believed in quiet diplomacy, not the loud, fanatical, empty posturing that grabs headlines because it's sensational. His way combined the quiet look of confidence with the voice of reason.

A president of the UN General Assembly called Mike Pearson "a great Canadian, who is one of the foremost citizens of the world." He said this because of Mike's pivotal role in the creation of the UN peacekeeping force. A special arm of the UN that Mike literally invented and urged into a reality, the peacekeeping force is a multinational army dedicated to protecting the peace wherever it might be needed. To this day, it's at work in trouble spots around the globe.

How did Mike come to be so dedicated to peace? He'd witnessed first-hand the horrors of combat, seen the lives of happy, gifted young men snuffed out by war. He himself had lived through years of war nerves—what is today called "post-traumatic stress syndrome."

Ever humble about his own personal accomplishments, Mike was quick to point out that every Canadian can make a difference in the world. He said, "No country in the world is more envied, and with such good reason, as Canada. No country has a greater destiny ahead if we wish to make it so . . . This is entirely our own, and no one else's responsibility."

Timeline: The life and times of Lester B. Pearson

YEAR		LESTER'S LIFE	EVENTS IN CANADA AND THE WORLD
1897		Lester is born on April 23 in Newtonbrook, Ontario (now part of Toronto).	Thousands of fortune seekers rush to the Yukon to find gold. Queen Victoria celebrates her diamond jubilee, marking 60 years of her reign.
1898		Lester's brother, Vaughn, is born.	The district of Yukon is organized as a separate territory. The United States declares war on Spain and captures the Philippines, Cuba, and Puerto Rico.
1913		Lester enrols at the University of Toronto to study history.	The Ford Motor Company begins the first moving assembly line in the world, making Model-T cars.
1914			World War I begins when Austria declares war on Serbia.
1915		Lester volunteers to serve with the University of Toronto hospital unit in Greece.	
1917		Lester (now renamed Mike) transfers to the Royal Flying Corps in Great Britain. He is hit by a bus in London, England.	The Halifax Explosion occurs: two ships (one loaded with explosives) collide in Halifax's harbour, killing 2,000 and badly damaging the city. The Russian Revolution begins with the ousting of Czar Nicholas II.
1918		Mike is declared unfit for flying and is sent home	
1919		Mike finishes his bachelor's degree. After articling for a week at a law firm, he plays semi-professional baseball and works in a meat-processing plant, then moves on to Chicago where he works as a clerk for the fertilizer division of the same company.	The Winnipeg General Strike occurs. The Treaty of Versailles is signed on June 28, officially ending World War I.
1920			Arthur Meighen becomes the ninth prime minister of Canada (1920–1921). Women become eligible to sit in the House of Commons. The Progressive party forms. The Royal North-West Mounted Police merges with the Dominion Police to become the Royal Canadian Mounted Police. The League of Nations is established.
1921		Mike wins a scholarship and enrols at Oxford University in England.	William Lyon Mackenzie King becomes the 10th prime minister of Canada (1921–1926) and secretary of state for external affairs. Agnes Macphail is the first woman elected to Parliament.
1923		Mike earns a master's degree in history from Oxford University. He becomes a lecturer in the history department of the University of Toronto.	Sir Frederick Banting and J. J. R. Macleod of the University of Toronto win the Nobel prize for medicine for the discovery of insulin to treat diabetes. The Munich Beer Putsch takes place: Adolf Hitler, together with General Erich Ludendorff, tries to overthrow the German government.
1925		Mike marries Maryon Moody.	
1926			Arthur Meighen begins his second term as the 9th prime minister. William Lyon Mackenzie King begins serving his second term as the 10th prime minister on September 25 (1926–1930).

More on the life and times of Lester B. Pearson

YEAR	LESTER'S LIFE	EVENTS IN CANADA AND THE WORLD
1927	Mike's son, Geoffrey Arthur Holland, is born.	The Old Age Pension Act is passed. The first public demonstration of television is given in Washington, DC, and New York.
1928	Mike accepts the position of first secretary in the Department of External Affairs.	Amelia Earhart becomes the first woman to fly across the Atlantic: she flies as a passenger in a plane that takes 24 hours 49 minutes.
1929	Mike's daughter, Patricia Lillian, is born.	The Judicial Committee of the Privy Council declares women to be legally "persons." The 10-year-long Great Depression begins.
1930	Mike participates in the London Naval Conference.	Richard B. Bennett becomes the 11th prime minister (1930–1935). Cairine Wilson is the first female to be appointed a senator.
1931	Mike acts as secretary of a commission on wheat futures.	The Statute of Westminster gives Canada the power to change its constitution, but it must still take place in the British parliament.
1932		The Co-operative Commonwealth Federation (CCF) party is founded.
1933	Mike attends the World Disarmament Conference in Geneva.	Adolf Hitler is appointed chancellor of Germany.
1934	Mike is secretary of a commission investigating grain prices.	Mao Zedong's Chinese Communist Army begins the 370-day, several-thousand-kilometre Long March to northern China.
1935	Mike is posted to the office of the High Commissioner for Canada in London, England, as the first secretary. He participates in another London Naval Conference, and in sessions of the League of Nations.	The Bank of Canada is formed. The RCMP stops the On-to-Ottawa Trek in Regina. William L. Mackenzie King begins his third term as prime minister. Tommy Douglas wins a seat in the House of Commons for the CCF party.
1938		The German army marches into Austria and annexes it to Germany.
1939		World War II begins on Sept. 3 as Britain declares war on Germany. Canada declares war on Germany on September 10.
1940		The National Resources Mobilization Act is introduced. White women are given the right to vote in Quebec. Canada declares war on Italy on June 10. Germany invades Holland, Belgium, Luxembourg, and France. Winston Churchill becomes prime minister of Great Britain.
1941	Mike returns to Ottawa.	Japan attacks Pearl Harbor, Hawaii. Canada, Great Britain, and the United States declare war on Japan.
1942	Mike is named minister-counsellor at the Canadian Legation in Washington, DC.	A national plebiscite on conscription is held. The Progressive and Conservative parties unite to become the Progressive Conservative (PC) party. Canada and the United States force citizens of Japanese descent to move away from the west coast.
1943	He chairs United Nations Relief and Rehabilitation Administration (UNRRA). He also becomes chair of the UN Interim Commission on Food and Agriculture.	Canadian troops invade Sicily, Italy.

Still more on the life and times of Lester B. Pearson

YEAR	LESTER'S LIFE	EVENTS IN CANADA AND THE WORLD
1944		Ottawa imposes limited conscription for overseas service. Allies land in Normandy, France on D-Day, June 6.
1945	Mike is promoted to the rank of ambassador. He participates in the San Francisco Conference to create the UN.	The Liberal party wins the postwar election. The family-allowance program (baby bonus) begins. Canada joins the United Nations (UN). Germany surrenders on May 8. The United States drops two atomic bombs on Japan. Japan surrenders on September 2. The Cold War begins (1945–1990).
1946	Mike returns to Ottawa and becomes undersecretary of state for external affairs. He heads the Canadian delegation to the UN until 1956.	The first meeting of the United Nations General Assembly takes place in London, England.
1947		The Canadian Citizenship Act is implemented. India and Pakistan gain independence from Great Britain.
1948	Mike runs for and wins a seat in the House of Commons in a by-election. He is named minister of external affairs.	William Lyon Mackenzie King resigns as prime minister. Louis St. Laurent becomes the 12th prime minister of Canada (1948–1957). South Africa introduces apartheid. A war (1948–1949) between Israel and Arab forces from Egypt, Syria, Transjordan (later Jordan), Lebanon, and Iraq begins.
1949	Mike signs the treaty for the creation of the North Atlantic Treaty Organization (NATO) and heads the Canadian delegation until 1957.	Newfoundland joins Canada. The Supreme Court becomes the last court of appeal.
1950		Former prime minister William Lyon Mackenzie King dies. The Korean War begins (1950–53).
1951	Mike chairs the NATO council.	The first colour television broadcast takes place in five US cities
1952	Mike becomes president of the UN General Assembly until 1953.	The CBC begins television broadcasts in French and English. King George VI dies and is succeeded by his daughter, who becomes Queen Elizabeth II.
1956	Mike proposes the solution to end the Suez War by sponsoring the creation of the United Nations Emergency Force to police that area.	The Suez War takes place: Great Britain and France attack Egypt to maintain international control of the Suez Canal.
1957	Mike wins the Nobel Peace Prize.	John Diefenbaker becomes the 13th prime minister of Canada. Ellen Fairclough becomes Canada's first female cabinet minister. The USSR launches the first two earth satellites: Sputnik I and II. The Vietnam War begins (1957–1975): North Vietnam forces attack South Vietnam and win control of it.
1958	Mike is elected leader of the Liberal party.	John Diefenbaker is re-elected as prime minister. Canada's first Bill of Rights is introduced in Parliament. James Gladstone is appointed Canada's first First Nations senator. Egypt and Syria form the short-lived United Arab Republic.
1959		The development of the Avro Arrow CF-105 supersonic, all-weather interceptor jet aircraft is cancelled. First Nations people are granted the right to vote.

Even more on the life and times of Lester B. Pearson

YEAR	LESTER'S LIFE	EVENTS IN CANADA AND THE WORLD
1960		The Canadian Bill of Rights is passed.
1961		The CCF party changes its name to the New Democratic Party. The Berlin Wall is built.
1962		The last execution takes place in Canada. US president Kennedy orders a naval blockade of Cuba, bringing the world to the brink of nuclear war.
1963	Mike becomes the 14th prime minister of Canada (1963–1968).	The Royal Commission on Bilingualism and Biculturalism begins. The FLQ begin bombing mailboxes in Quebec. US president Kennedy is assassinated on Nov. 23 in Dallas, Texas.
1964		Nelson Mandela is jailed for opposing apartheid in South Africa.
1965	Mike wins his second term as prime minister.	The Maple Leaf flag is adopted. The Canada Pension Plan is established.
1966		Universal medical care is granted. The CBC begins colour television broadcasts. Indira Gandhi becomes prime minister of India.
1967		Canada celebrates the 100th anniversary of Confederation. The World Exposition takes place in Montreal. French president Charles de Gaulle visits Montreal and exclaims *Vive le Québec libre* ("Long live free Quebec"). Israel fights Egypt, Jordan, and Syria in the Six Day War.
1968	Mike retires as leader of the Liberal party. He becomes chancellor of and lecturer of history and political science at Carleton University in Ottawa. He is invested as a Companion of the Order of Canada.	Pierre Elliott Trudeau becomes the 15th prime minister of Canada. Lincoln MacCauley Alexander becomes the first black MP. René Lévesque founds the separatist Parti Québécois. US civil rights leader Martin Luther King is assassinated.
1969		Parliament and federal institutions are made officially bilingual when the Official Languages Act becomes law. New Brunswick becomes first province to be officially bilingual. US astronaut Neil Armstrong becomes the first person to walk on the moon.
1970	Mike is diagnosed with cancer.	Front de libération du Québec (FLQ) terrorists kidnap two political officials. The War Measures Act is passed, suspending civil liberties. Floods kill 500,000 in east Pakistan.
1971	The annual Lester B. Pearson Award is created to honour the National Hockey League's outstanding player in the regular season.	Fighting against the West Pakistani army, India invades East Pakistan, which becomes the independent country of Bangladesh.
1972	Mike publishes the first of three volumes of his memoirs, *Mike: The memoirs of the right honourable Lester B. Pearson, 1897–1948.* He dies of cancer in Ottawa on December 27.	Muriel McQueen Fergusson is appointed the first female speaker of the Senate. Ceylon changes its name to Sri Lanka.

Glossary: Words and facts you might want to know

air-raid siren: a device that makes loud sounds to warn about approaching air raids from an enemy and to indicate when the danger has passed.

ambassador: a diplomat who serves as the official representative of his or her own country in a foreign country.

Black Thursday: October 24, 1929, the official beginning of the stock-market crash of 1929. The value of stocks on the New York Stock Exchange dropped dramatically when too many people tried to sell them at the same time. On that day, $9 billion of stock value was lost. Eleven people were so upset about it, they threw themselves out of skyscraper windows. Prices continued to drop over the next week. This was one of the causes of the Great Depression, which lasted 10 years.

British Commonwealth: an association of Great Britain and its former colonies. It is a voluntary organization of countries that have pledged to work together to improve world peace, social understanding, racial equality, and economic development. Canada was the first colony to become independent of Great Britain in 1867.

cabinet minister: a member of the legislature (House of Commons or the Senate) who has been invited by the prime minister to head a major government department or ministry of state. The cabinet acts as a unit; any opinion expressed by a minister is that of the whole cabinet.

Canada Pension Plan (CPP): since 1966, payments made to people who have retired from working. The government collects money for this program from people who are working.

Churchill, Sir Winston Leonard Spencer (1874–1965): British prime minister (1940–45, 1951–55) who led the British people during World War II from near-defeat to victory.

civil servant: a person who works for the government. Examples of civil servants include teachers, trash collectors, mail carriers, and public library staff.

civil service: the group of non-elected people who are hired to work in the administration of a country at a local or national level. This excludes those who are employed for military purposes.

coat of arms: the arrangement of official symbols for a family, state, et cetera, that are usually placed on and around a shield. The symbols tell some of the history and notable achievements of the family or state.

Confederation: on July 1, 1867, the joining together of the British colonies of New Brunswick, Nova Scotia, and Canada (the colony formed in 1841 from what were then the Lower and Upper Canada colonies). The resulting country was named the Dominion of Canada.

Conservative Party of Canada: the first party to govern the Dominion of Canada. It began in 1854 when politicians from Upper and Lower Canada joined to form a coalition government for the Province of Canada. It was initially called the Liberal-Conservative party, but changed its name to the Conservative party around the time of Confederation, when a separate Liberal party was formed. Sir John A. Macdonald was its first leader.

corps company: an army unit usually consisting of two or more divisions.

Diefenbaker, John George (1895–1979): Canada's 13th prime minister (1957–1963). Born in Ontario but raised in Saskatchewan from the age of seven, he practised law before entering politics. He was a member of the Progressive Conservative party. His efforts resulted in the Canadian Bill of Rights and First Nations peoples' right to vote in federal elections.

Dominion Day: term used until recently for July 1, the day on which Canada celebrates the anniversary of Confederation. On this day in 1867, Canada was given semi-independence as a "dominion," not a fully independent state. Independence came in 1931, but this event is not celebrated.

Expo '67: the 1967 International and Universal Exposition, a world's fair that was held in Montreal to coincide with the Canadian centennial. Expo '67 opened on April 28, 1967, and featured 90 pavilions for nations, corporations, and industries. It closed on October 29, after six months and 50 million visitors. Canada had a population of 20 million at the time.

feminist: someone who believes that women should have the same opportunities as men.

governor general: the representative of the king or queen in Canada who provides the royal assent necessary for all laws passed by Parliament. The gover-

More words and facts you might want to know

nor general is a figurehead who performs only symbolic, formal, ceremonial, and cultural duties, and whose job is to encourage Canadian excellence, identity, unity, and leadership. Governors general are Canadian citizens appointed for terms of approximately five years. During their term, they live and work in the official residence of Rideau Hall in Ottawa, parts of which are open to the public as a historic site, art gallery, and educational centre.

Great Depression (1929–1939): also known as "The Dirty Thirties," this was a worldwide economic slump. The cause is still being debated by experts. Two catastrophes happened right before the Depression: an enormous loss of the wheat crop in 1928 and the stock-market crash in October 1929. Many people were out of work and money and food supplies began to run low. The Depression affected everyone in some manner, and there was no way to escape it. As the Depression carried on, one in five Canadians became dependent on government relief. Unemployment ran as high as 30 per cent of the labour force.

Hitler, Adolf (1889–1945): ruled Germany as dictator from 1933 to 1945. Although born in Austria, he considered himself German. After he led the Nazi party to power in 1933, he prepared the country for war. World War II began in 1939 and ended a week after he killed himself, in 1945. He was responsible for the deaths of millions of people in the concentration camps that he set up.

House of Commons: the lower house of Parliament. It consists of a speaker, the prime minister and his cabinet, members of the governing party, members of the opposition parties, and sometimes a few independent members (elected members who do not belong to an official party). The members of the House (called members of Parliament or MPs) are elected in constituency elections or by-elections by the Canadian people. The House (often incorrectly referred to as Parliament) is important because it is where all new laws start.

international diplomacy: the art and practice of conducting negotiations among people who represent their countries or other groups. Things like peace, war, culture, economics, and trade are often the subject of negotiations between diplomats. It is very important to be skilled at phrasing sentences in a non-confrontational or social manner.

King George VI (1895–1952): king of Great Britain (1936–1952) and father of Great Britain's current Queen Elizabeth II. He assumed the throne unexpectedly when his brother, King Edward VIII, abdicated (quit). He served in the navy during World War I and was king during World War II. He visited troops in Europe and North Africa during the war. As German bombs fell on London, he and his family remained in London at Buckingham Palace.

King, William Lyon Mackenzie (1874–1950): Canada's 10th prime minister (1921–1926, 1926–1930, 1935–1948). He was born and raised in Berlin (now Kitchener), Ontario. He was the grandson of Upper Canadian rebel William Lyon Mackenzie. His interest in labour drew him to working as a mediator to resolve disputes between workers and management. He led Canada during World War II.

LaMarsh, Julia Verlyn (Judy) (1924–1980): lawyer and Liberal MP (1960–1968). Serving under Prime Minister Lester Pearson, she was only the second female federal cabinet minister in Canadian history, and the first to serve in a Liberal cabinet. As minister of national health and welfare (1963–1965), she introduced the Canada Pension Plan and designed the medicare system. As secretary of state (1965–1968), Judy established the Royal Commission on the Status of Women in Canada. She also served as minister of amateur sport from 1963 to 1965.

League of Nations (1919–1945): international organization of (eventually) 63 countries established after World War I at the Paris Peace Conference. The intention of the league was to help countries resolve arguments peacefully and avoid future wars. However, it was not able to stop World War II from starting. It was replaced by the United Nations.

Liberal Party of Canada: political party that adopted its name in 1867, after Confederation. It was formed from the union of the pre-Confederation Reform party (hailing from what is now called Ontario) and Parti rouge (from what is now called Quebec).

Massey, Charles Vincent (1887–1967): Canada's first Canadian-born governor general (1952–1959). He was a lecturer in modern history at the University of Toronto from 1913 until 1915. He served as Canada's first diplomatic representative in the United

More words and facts you might want to know

States (1926–1930) and as Canada's high commissioner in Great Britain (1935–1946). His efforts after the war resulted in the government providing financial support for Canadian arts, humanities, and social sciences, creating a national library, and financially aiding universities.

medicare: unofficial name of Canada's universal public-health-insurance system. It provides services to all Canadians no matter what their income level is. According to the Canada Health Act, the provinces give all residents health-insurance cards, which allow each person to receive free medical care for almost all procedures. People can choose their own doctor, hospital, et cetera.

minority government: when the political party in power has more MPs than each individual party in opposition but less than the total of all the opposition MPs.

modern history: the study of past events from the end of the Middle Ages, around 1650, to today. Its exact definition depends on the specific usage. Some people say it ended anywhere from the 1960s to the early 1980s, when postmodernism began.

Moody, Maryon Elspeth (1902–1991): wife of Lester Bowles Pearson. They met at the University of Toronto, where he was one of her teachers. They married in 1925 and had a son, Geoffrey, and a daughter, Patricia.

Nasser, Gamal Abdel (1918–1970): second president of Egypt (1954–1970). He took part in overthrowing the British regime and the Egyptian royal family in 1952. He started the Suez War when he seized control of the Suez Canal from the French and British. He died of a sudden heart attack while negotiating a settlement following Egypt's defeat by Israel in the Six Day War of 1967.

Nazis: an abbreviation used for members of the National Socialist German Workers' Party, which was in power in Germany from 1933 to 1945 under Adolf Hitler. The party beliefs were strongly anti-communist, anti-Semitic, and racist. Hitler was committed to expanding Germany.

New Democratic Party (NDP): a national political party that was founded in 1961 when the Co-operative Commonwealth Federation (CCF) merged with unions within the Canadian Labour Congress. The CCF wanted to get better results in elections; the unions wanted an official way to become involved in politics. While it has yet to be in power federally, the NDP has formed governments in Ontario, British Columbia, Yukon, Saskatchewan, and Manitoba.

Nobel Peace Prize: since 1901, an award given by the Norwegian parliament to people or institutions to acknowledge excellence in promoting world peace. Funds for the awards come from an endowment by Alfred Nobel (1833–1896), the Swedish inventor of dynamite. Awards are also given for physics, chemistry, medicine, and literature. The Swedish bank began the Nobel Prize for economics in 1969.

North Atlantic Treaty Organization (NATO): since 1949, a group of countries that have agreed to defend each other militarily. Canada, the United States, Great Britain, and the countries of Western Europe united to prevent the spread of communism and the expansion of the Soviet Union.

Order of the British Empire (OBE): award of honour created during World War I by George V to recognize people from Great Britain and other countries who helped the British war effort both as combatants and as civilians on the home front. Since the war ended, the award has also recognized service to the arts and sciences, public services outside the civil service, and work with charities.

Parliament Hill: site of Canada's federal government buildings in Ottawa, Ontario. The House of Commons, the Senate, the offices of many members of Parliament, and committee rooms are housed here. It is a complex of buildings that sits above the Ottawa River. Construction began in 1859, and it was officially opened in 1866. It was destroyed by a fire and rebuilt in 1916.

Pentagon: headquarters of the US Department of Defense in Arlington, Virginia. It is a huge, five-sided building.

points system: introduced in 1967, a method of selecting independent immigrants who apply to come to Canada. It was incorporated into immigration regulations to remove discrimination based on nationality or race, and other unfair practices that were used to select newcomers. In the points system, immigration officers assign points in each of several categories, such as education, job opportunities in Canada, years of work experience, age, relatives already in Canada, and degree of

Still more words and facts you might want to know

fluency in English or French. Independent immigrants must have a certain minimum number of total points (e.g., 67 out of 100).

Red Ensign: flag of Canada before 1965, when it was replaced by the Maple Leaf. It is now the official flag of Ontario and Manitoba.

Roosevelt, Franklin Delano (1882–1945): 32nd president of the United States (1933–1945). When he took office for the first of his four terms, the United States was in the midst of the Great Depression. To combat the situation, he introduced many policy changes, which were called "the New Deal." From 1941, he directed the United States' involvement in World War II and died as the war was coming to a close.

royal commission: an official inquiry into matters of public concern. The cabinet receives formal approval from the governor general to order the commission. Witnesses are called to testify, documents are gathered, and experts are hired to investigate the subject of the inquiry.

St. Laurent, Louis (1882–1973): Canada's 12th prime minister (1948–1957). In 1941, while working as a lawyer in Quebec, he was invited by William Lyon Mackenzie King to become minister of justice. He became King's successor as leader of the Liberal party. He sent Canadian troops to fight for the United Nations in Korea.

Social Credit party: a former federal party. It still exists as a provincial party in British Columbia. From 1935 to 1968, the federal Social Credit party sent members to Parliament, mainly from Alberta, British Columbia, and Quebec. It believed that the government should give people money so they could afford to purchase goods and services available in the community. This money was called "social credit."

Suez War (1956): a crisis that arose when Egyptian president Nasser took control of the Suez Canal and threatened to charge huge tolls after the United States and Great Britain withdrew their offer to help pay for Aswan High Dam on the Nile River. Israel, Great Britain, and France invaded Egypt to restore international control of the canal. A UN police force restored peace.

Trudeau, Pierre Elliott (1919–2000): 15th prime minister of Canada (1968–1979, 1980–1984). Pierre worked as a lawyer and law professor before he entered politics in 1965.

Union Jack: or the Union Flag, the national flag of the United Kingdom. It combines the emblems of the three countries united under one sovereign: the kingdoms of England and Wales, Scotland, and Ireland.

United Nations (UN): an organization that works for international peace and security. The UN provides a place for representatives of countries to meet and settle their problems peacefully. It was established in 1945, at the end of World War II. Its headquarters are in New York City. Another office is in Geneva, Switzerland, and agencies can be found throughout the world. Fifty-one countries joined the UN when it started (including Canada and the United States) and over 70 more have signed on since.

Vietnam War (1954–1975): a conflict that began with the military defeat of the French in their former colony of Vietnam. This was followed by communist North Vietnamese invading South Vietnam in hopes of reuniting the country. Fearing the spread of communism throughout the world, the United States sent troops to support the South Vietnamese army. US troops pulled out following the signing of the 1973 Paris Peace Accord. South Vietnam fell to the North when an armed revolt in the South was crushed following the North's refusal to hold free and democratic elections as had been promised.

World War I (1914–1918): also known as the First World War, or the Great War. It was an international conflict that involved most of the countries of Europe as well as Russia, the United States, the Middle East, and other regions. The war pitted the Central Powers—mainly Germany, Austria-Hungary, and Turkey—against the Allies—mainly France, Great Britain (including Canada), Russia, Italy, Japan, and, from 1917, the United States. It ended with the defeat of the Central Powers.

World War II (1939–1945): also called the Second World War, a conflict that involved almost every part of the world. The main participants were the Axis powers—Germany, Italy, and Japan—and the Allies—France, Great Britain (including Canada and Australia), the United States, and Russia. The war was a continuation of problems left unresolved by World War I (1914–1918). It was the largest war in history and ended with the defeat of the Axis countries.

Index